ELEMENTS OF THE QABALAH

ELIPHAS LÉVI

TABLE OF CONTENTS

ELEMENTS OF THE QABALAH

IN TEN LESSONS

LETTERS OF ELIPHAS LÉVI

FIRST LESSON

GENERAL PROLEGOMENA

Friend and Brother,

I can give you this title because you are searching for the truth in the sincerity of your heart, ready to make the necessary sacrifices in order to find it.

Truth, being the essence of all that is, is not difficult to find: it is within us and we are within it. It is like light and the blind do not see it.

Being is. This is incontestable and absolute. The exact idea of Being is truth; its knowledge is science; its ideal expression is reason; its activity is creation and justice.

You wish to believe, you say. For this, it is enough to know and to love truth. For the true faith is the unshakeable adhesion of the mind to the necessary deductions of science in conjectural infinity.

Only occult sciences give certitude, for they have their bases in realities and not in dreams.

In every religious symbol, they bring out the true and the false. What is true is the same everywhere, but falsehoods spring up according to places, times and people.

These sciences are three: the Qabalah, Magic and Hermeticism.

The Qabalah, or traditional science of the Hebrews, might be called the mathematics of human thought. It is (he algebra of faith. It solves all problems of the soul as equations, by isolating the unknowns. It gives to ideas the clarity and rigorous exactitude of numbers; its results, for the mind, are infallibility (always relative, however, to the sphere of human knowledge) and for the heart, profound peace.

Magic, or the science of the magi, has its ancient representatives in the disciples, and perhaps the teachers, of Zoroaster. It is the knowledge of secret and particular laws of nature which produce hidden forces, magnets and loadstones which may exist even outside the realm of metal. In a word, and to use a modern expression, it is the science of universal magnetism.

Hermeticism is the science of nature hidden in the hieroglyoics and symbols of the ancient world. It is the search for the principle of life, along with the dream (for those who have not yet achieved it) of accomplishing the great work, that is the reproduction by man of the divine, natural fire which creates and recreates beings.

Here, my friend, are the things you desire to study. The circle they enclose is immense, but the principles are so simple that they are represented and contained in the signs of the numbers and in the letters of the alphabet. 'It is a labour of Hercules that is also a child *s game,' say the masters of holy science.

Characteristics necessary to success in this study are a great rectitude of judgment and a great independence of mind. One must rid oneself of all prejudice and every preconceived notion, and it is for this reason that Christ said: "Unless you become as a little child, you cannot enter the Malkouht," that is, the kingdom of knowledge.

We will begin with the Qabalah, whose divisions are these; Berechith, Mercavah, Gematria and Lemurah.

Yours in the holy science,

Eliphas Lévi

SECOND LESSON

THE QABALAH - GOAL AND METHOD

In studying the Qabalah, one should strive to arrive at profound peace by means of tranquillity of mind and peace of heart.

Tranquillity of mind is an effect of certainty; peace of heart comes from patience and faith.

Without faith, science leads to doubt; without science, faith leads to superstition. Uniting them brings certainty, but in so doing they must never be confused with each other. The object of faith is hypothesis, and this becomes certitude when the hypothesis is necessitated by evidence or by the demonstrations of science.

Science establishes facts. From the repetition of facts, it presupposes laws. The generality of facts in the presence of such and such a force demonstrates the existence of laws. Intelligent laws are necessarily imposed and governed by intelligence. Unity within the laws presupposes the unity of legislative intelligence. This intelligence, which we are forced to imagine, only seeing it at work in external manifestations, and which we can in no way define, is what we call God!

You receive my letter; there is an obvious fact. You recognize my handwriting and my thoughts and you conclude from this that it is indeed I who have written to you. This is a reasonable hypothesis, but the necessary hypothesis is that someone wrote the letter. It could be counterfeit, though you have no reason to suppose it is. Were you to suppose so, groundlessly, you would be making a very doubtful hypothesis. Were you to claim that the letter, fully written, fell from the sky, you would be making an absurd hypothesis.

Here is, then, according to Qabalistic method, how certitude is formed;

Evidence	
Scientific demonstration	certitude
Necessary hypothesis	
Reasonable hypothesis	probability
Doubtful hypothesis	doubt
Absurd hypothesis	error

By keeping to this method, the mind acquires a veritable infallibility, for it affirms what it knows, believes what it must necessarily suppose, admits reasonable suppositions, examines doubtful ones, and rejects those which are absurd.

All the Qabalah is contained in what the masters call the thirty-two roads and the fifty gates. The thirty-two roads are thirty-two absolute and real ideas attached to the signs of the ten arithmetical numbers and to the twenty-two letters of the Hebraic alphabet.

Here are these ideas:

NUMBERS

1 Supreme power	6 Beauty
2 Absolute wisdom	7 Victory
3 Infinite intelligence	8 Eternity
4 Goodness	9 Productivity
5 Justice or harshness	10 Reality

LETTERS

Aleph	Father
Lamed	Sacrifice
Beth	Mother
Mem	Death
Gimel	Nature
Nun	Reversibility
Daleth	Authority
Samekh	Universal being
He	Religion
Pe	Immortality
Vav	Liberty
Ayin	Balance
Zayin	Ownership
Sadhe	Shadow and reflection
Cheth	Distribution
Koph	Light
Teth	Prudence
Resh	Recognition
Yod	Order
Tav	Synthesis
Kaph	Force

THIRD LESSON

USE OF THE METHOD

In the preceding lesson I spoke only of the thirty-two roads; later I will talk of the fifty gates.

The ideas expressed by numbers and letters are incontestable realities. These ideas follow from one another and agree like the numbers, themselves. One proceeds logically from one to the next. Man is the son of woman, but woman comes out of man as number comes out of unity. Woman clarifies nature, nature reveals authority, which creates religion, basis for liberty, which makes man master of himself and of the universe, etc . . . (Get hold of a Tarot - I believe in fact you already have one - and, in two series, lay out the ten allegorical cards numbered from one to twenty-one. You will see all the figures which correspond to the letters. As for the numbers from one to ten, you will find them repeated four times with the symbols of the baton or sceptre of (he father, the cup or *délices* of the mother, the sword of love and (he coins of productivity. The Tarot is included in the hieroglyphic book of the thirty-two roads, and its summary explanation can be found in the book attributed to the patriarch, Abraham, which is called *Sepher-Jezirah*.

The savant Court de Gebelin was the first to discover the importance of the Tarot, which is the great key to the hieratic hieroglyphs. Its symbols and numbers are to be found in the prophecies of Ezekiel and of St John. The Bible is an inspired book, but the Tarot is the book of inspiration. It has also been called the wheel, *rota*, whence *tarot* and *torah*. The ancient Rosicrucians knew it well and the Marquis de Suchet speaks of it in his book on visionaries.

It is from this book that our card games have come. Spanish cards still bear the principal signs of the primitive Tarot and they are used to play the game of the *hombre* or man, vague reminiscence of the early use of a mysterious book, containing oracular decrees about all human divinities.

The earliest Tarots were medals which have since become talismans. The *clavicules* or little keys of Solomon were made up of thirty-six talismans bearing seventy-two engravings analogous to the hieroglyphic figures of the Tarot. These figures, altered by copyists, can still be found on ancient *clavicules* which exist in some libraries. A manuscript of this type exists in the Bibliothéque Nationale and another in the Bibliothéque de l'Arsenal. The only authentic manuscripts of the *clavicules* are those which give the series of thirty-six talismans with the seventy-two mysterious names; the others, however ancient they may be, belong to fantasies of black magic and contain nothing more than clever tricks.

For an explanation of the Tarot, see my Dogma and Ritual of True Magic.

Yours in the holy science,
Eliphas Lévi

FOURTH LESSON

THE QABALAH I

Brother and Friend,

Bereschith means 'genesis'; Mercavah means 'chariot', alluding to the wheels and mysterious animals of Ezekiel.

The Bereschith and the Mercavah summarize the science of God and of the world.

I say 'science of God', and yet God is infinitely unknowable. His nature entirely escapes our investigations. He is the absolute principle of beitig and of beings and must not be confused with the effects he produces; and it can be said, affirming his existence all the while, that he is neither being nor a being. Such a definition confounds reason, without however causing us to go astray, and keeps us for ever from all idolatry.

God is the only absolute *postulatum* of all

science, the entirely necessary hypothesis which serves as a basis for any certainty; and here is how our ancient masters established, above science itself, this assured hypothesis of faith: Being is. In Being is life. Life is made manifest by movement. Movement is perpetuated by the balancing of forces. Harmony results from the analogy of opposites. There are, in nature, an immutable law and an undefinable progress. A perpetual changing of forms and the indestructability of substance, this is what one finds upon observing the physical world.

Metaphysics presents us with analogous laws and facts either in an intellectual or a moral order, on one side unchanging truth, on the other, fantasy and imagination. On one side there is goodness which is truth, on the other, evil, which is false and from these apparent conflicts arise both judgment and virtue. Virtue is composed of goodness and justice. Its goodness makes it indulgent. Its justice makes it harsh. Good because it is just and just because it is good: it is always beautiful.

This great harmony of the physical and moral worlds, incapable of having a cause superior to itself, reveals and demonstrates to us the existence of an unchanging wisdom and of an infinitely active creative intelligence.

Upon this widom and tins intelligence, each inseparable from the other reposes the supreme power which the Hebrews have named the crown. The crown and not the king, for the idea of a king would imply an idol. For Qabalists, the supreme power is the crown of the universe and the entirety of creation is the kingdom, or if you prefer, the domain of this crown.

No one can give what he has not, thus we can assume that what we see manifested in effects is also present in the cause.

God, then, is the supreme power or crown (Kether) which sits upon immutable wisdom (Chokmah) and creative intelligence (Binah); in him are goodness (Hesed) and justice (Geburah) which are the ideal of beauty (Tiphereth). In him are for ever victorious movement (Netzach) and the great eternal rest (Hod). His desire is a continual giving of life (Yesod) and his kingdom (Malkuth) is the immensity which populates the universe.

Enough; we are acquainted with God!
Yours in the holy science,

Eliphas Lévi

FIFTH LESSON

THE QABALAH II

Brother and Friend,

This rational conscience of divinity, spread over the ten ciphers which compose all numbers, give you the whole method of Qabalistic philosophy. This method is composed of thirty-two means or instruments of knowledge which are called the thirty-two roads, and of fifty subjects to which the science may be applied and that are called the fifty gates.

Universal synthetic science is thus regarded as a temple to which there lead thirty-two paths and which may be entered through thirty-two doors.

This numerical system, which could also be called decimal since it is based on the number ten, establishes by means of analogies an exact classification of all human knowledge. Nothing is more ingenious, but likewise nothing is more logical and exact.

This number ten applied to absolute notions of being in the divine order, in the metaphysical order and in the natural order is thus repeated three times which gives thirty for purposes of analysis; add syllepsis and synthesis that is, unity which begins as a concept in the mind and unity which brings together as one all that is, and you have thirty-two roads.

The fifty gates are a classification of all being into five series of ten each and which embraces all one can know and extends into the entire body of knowledge.

But it is not enough to have found an exact mathematical method; in order to be perfect, this method must be progressively revelatory, that is, it must give us the means of making all possible deductions unerringly, of obtaining new knowledge and of developing the mind without leaving anything to the capriciousness of the imagination.

This is what one obtains through the Gematria and the Lemurah, which are the mathematics of idea. The Qabalah has its ideal geometry, its philosophical algebra and its analogic trigonometry. It is thus that, so to speak, it obliges nature to render up her secrets.

Once such high knowledge is acquired, one goes on to the final revelations of the transcendental Qabalah, studying in the schememamphorash the source and reason of all dogmas.

There, brother and friend, is what there is for you to lean. Does it frighten you? My letters are short, but concise, and say much. I have spaced my first five lessons rather far apart so as to give you time for reflection. I can write to you more often if you so desire.

With the ardent wish of being useful to you, I remain, your devoted servant in the holy science,

Eliphas Lévi

SIXTH LESSON

THE QABALAH III

Brother and Friend,

The Bible gives man two names. The first is Adam, which means 'drawn from the earth' or 'man of earth'; the second is Enos or Enoch, which means 'divine man' or 'lifted to God'. According to Genesis it is Enos who first spoke publicly on the principal of beings and this same Enos was, it is said, taken up alive into heaven after having engraved the primitive elements of religion and universal science on two stones which are called the columns or pillars of Enoch.

This Enoch is not a person, but a personification of humanity uplifted by religion and science to a sense of immortality. At the time designated by the name of Enos or Enoch, the cult of God appears on earth and ritual worship begins. This rime also marks the beginning of civilization with writing and the hieratic movements.

The civilizing genius which the Hebrews personify in Enoch was named Trismegistus by the Egyptians, and by the Greeks, Kadmos or Cadmus, he who saw the living stones of Thebes rise of themselves and take their place to the accompaniment of Amphion's lyre.

The primitive sacred book, the book that Postel calls the genesis of Enoch, is the first source of the Qabalah, tradition at once divine, human and religious. Here in all its simplicity appears the revelation of supreme intelligence to reason and to the love of man, the eternal law governing infinite expansion, the numbers in infinite expansion, the numbers in immensity and immensity in numbers, poetry in mathematics and mathematics in poetry.

Who would believe that the book which inspired all these theories and religious symbols has been preserved, coming down to us in the form of a deck of strange cards? Nothing is truer, however, and Court de

Gebelin, since followed by all those who have seriously studied the symbolism of these cards, was the first to discover it, in the last century.

The alphabet and the ten numerical signs are of course the basic elements of all sciences. Add to them the signs of the four cardinal points of heaven or of the four seasons and you have the book of Enoch in its entirety. But each sign represents an absolute or, if you will, essential idea.

The form of each cipher and of each letter has its mathematical reason and hieroglyphic significance. Ideas, inseparable from numbers, follow their movement, by addition, multiplication, etc., and acquire their exactitude.

The book of Enoch is the arithmetic of thought.

Yours in the holy science,

Eliphas Lévi

SEVENTH LESSON

THE QABALAH IV

Brother and Friend,

In the twenty-two keys of the Tarot, Court de Gebelin saw the representation of Egyptian mysteries and attributed their invention to Hermes Trismegistus, who was also called Thoth. It is certain that the hieroglyphs of the Tarot can be found on the ancient monuments of Egypt; it is certain that the signs of this book, traced in synoptic ensembles on steles or metal tables similar to the Isiac table of Bembo, were separately reproduced on engraved stones or medals which later became amulets and talismans. Thus the pages of the infinite book were separated into diverse combinations in order to assemble, transpose and re-transpose them for the obtaining of inexhaustible oracles of truth,

I have in my possession one of these ancient talismans which a traveling friend brought me from Egypt. It shows the two of coins, the figurative expression of the great law of polarity and equilibrium, producing harmony through the analogy of opposites. Here is how this symbol is shown in the Tarot which we possess and which is sold today. The medallion I have is rather worn, about as big as a silver five-franc piece, but thicker. The two polaric points are shown exactly as in our Italian Tarot, a lotus flower with a halo.

The astral current which separates and at the same time attracts the two polaric seats is represented on our Egyptian talisman by the Goat of Mendes placed between two vipers analogous to the serpents of the caducous. On the reverse side, one sees an adept or Egyptian priest who, having substituted himself for Mendes between the two points of universal equilibrium, is leading the goat, now simply a docile animal governed by man the imitator of God, down a long avenue planted with trees.

The ten numerical signs, the twenty-two letters of the alphabet and the four astronomical signs of the seasons are the summary of the entire Qabalah.

Twenty-two letters and ten numbers give the thirty-two ways of the Sepher Jetzirah; four gives the mercavah and the shememamphorash.

It is as simple as a child's game and as complicated as the most arduous problem of pure mathematics.

It is as profound and naive as truth and nature.

These four elementary, astronomical signs are the four forms of the sphinx and the four animals of Ezekiel and St John.

Yours in the holy science,

Eliphis Lévi

EIGHTH LESSON

THE QABALAH V

Brother and Friend,

The science of the Qabalah makes doubt, as regards religion, impossible, for it alone reconciles reason with faith by showing that universal dogma, at bottom always and everywhere the same, though formulated differently in   certain times and places, is the purest expression of the aspirations of the human mind, enlightened by a necessary faith. It points out the usefulness of religious practices which fortify will by fixing the attention, throwing light on all the cults. It proves that the most effective cult is that which brings together, so to speak, divinity and man, making him see it, touch it and incorporate it into himself.

It is enough to say that I am speaking here of the Catholic religion.

This religion, to the vulgar mind, appears to be the most absurd of all, for it is the most revealed; I use the word in its veritable sense, rewlare, to re-veil, to veil again. You know that, according to the Gospels, at the death of Christ the veil of the temple was rent asunder, and all down the ages the Church has worked dogmatically to weave a new one.

It is true that the heads of the sanctuary, themselves, having wished to become its princes, long ago lost the keys of high initiation. This does not, however, prevent the letter of dogma from being sacred, nor the sacraments from having their effect. I have set forth in my books that the Christian-Catholic cult is high magic organized and regularized by symbolism and hierarchy. It is a safety device offered to human weakness so as to fortify the desire for good.

Nothing has been forgotten, neither the dark mysterious temple, nor the incense, both calming and exalting, nor the long monotonous chants which rock the brain into a kind of semi-somnambulism. The dogma, whose obscure formulae appear to be the despair of all reason, serves as a barrier to the quibblings of inexperienced and indiscreet criticism. These formulae seem incomprehensible so as to better represent infinity. The mass itself, celebrated in a language which most of the people do not understand, gives width to the thought of he who officiates and allows him to satisfy, through prayer, all the needs of his mind and heart. This is why the Catholic religion resembles this sphinx of the fable who, century after century, becomes its own successor, always arising from its ashes; this great mystery of faith is simply a mystery of nature.

It would seem an enormous paradox were one to say that the Catholic religion is the only one which can justifiably be called natural, and yet, this is true, for it alone satisfies with any fullness at all this natural need of man, which is the religious sense.

Yours in the holy science,

Eliphas Levi

NINTH LESSON

THE QABALAH VI

Brother and Friend,

If the Catholic-Christian dogma is entirely Qabalisric, the same must be said for the great religions of the ancient world. The legend of Krishna as it is recounted in the Bhagavadam, is a veritable Gospel, similar to ours, but more naive, more brilliant. The incarnations of Vishnu number ten like the Sephiroth of the Qabalah and in some ways form a more complete revelation than ours. Osiris killed by Typhon, then resurrected by Isis, is Christ denied by the Jews, then honoured in the person of his mother. The *Thebaid* is a great religious epic which must be placed beside the great symbol of Prometheus. Antigone is as pure a type of divine woman as Mary. Everywhere good triumphs through voluntary sacrifice, after having been temporarily subjected to the wild assaults of evil. Even the rites are symbolic and are transmitted from one religion to another. Diadems, mitres, surplices belong to all the great religions. And so the conclusion is that all of them are false; whereas it is only this conclusion which is fake. The truth is that religion, like humanity, is one, always progressing, always changing, always the same. If, with the Egyptians, Jesus Christ is named Osiris, for the Scandinavians, Osiris is named Balder. He is killed by the wolf, Jeuris, but Odin calls him back to life, and the Valkyries themselves serve him hydromel in Valhalla. The skalds, the druids, the bards sing of the death and resurrection of Tarenis or of Tetenus, distribute to their faithful a sprig of holy mistletoe as we dispense the sacred palm during feasts of the summer solstice, and maintain a cult to virginity inspired by the priestesses of the isle of Seyne.

We can then, in all fair conscience, set about performing the duties imposed on us by our native religion. Religious practices are collective acts, repeated with direct, persevering intention. Such acts are always useful in that they strengthen the will, they are in a sense its gymnastics, and they bring us eventually to the spiritual goal which we wish to attain. Magic practices have the same end and give results analogous to religious practices, but less perfect.

How many men do not have the energy to do what they would like and what they ought to do? And there are such great numbers of women who devote themselves unflaggingly to labours as repugnant as those of the hospital or of teaching! Where do they find such strength? In small repeated religious practices. Each day they say their rosary, kneeling in prayer.

Yours in the holy science,

Eliphas Lévi

TENTH LESSON

THE QABALAH VII

Brother and Friend,

Religion is not a servitude imposed on man, but an aid which has been offered him. From time immemorial, sacerdotal castes have sought to exploit, sell and transform this aid into an unbearable yoke and burden; and the evangelical work of Jesus had as its aim the separation of the priest from religion, or at least, the return of the priest to his place as the minister, the servant of religion, by giving back to human consciousness all its liberty and reason. Look at the parable of the Good Samaritan and at these precious words: the law was made for man and not man for the law.

Woe to you who lay upon others burdens you would not so much as touch with the tip of your finger, etc. The official Church which declares itself infallible in the Apocalypse, the Qabalistic key to the Gospels, has always existed side by side with occult strains of Christianity that maintained an interpretation of dogma quite different from that given out to the vulgar.

The Templars, the Rosicrucians, the Freemasons of high grade, all belonged, before the French Revolution, to that church which counted among its apostles Pasqualis Marrincz, Saint-Martin and even Mme de Krudemer.

The distinctive characteristic of this school is to avoid publicity and never to grow into what might be referred to as a 'dissident sect'. The count Joseph de Maistre, this radical Catholic, was far more sympathetic than one might think to the society of the Martinistes, thus announcing an impending regeneration of dogma through the lights which shine forth from the sanctuaries of occultism. There exist today fervent priests initiated into antique doctrine and one bishop among others has just died who asked me for Qabalistic information. The disciples of Saint-Martin called themselves the unknown philosophers, and now other disciples of a modern master, fortunate enough to remain anonymous, need take no name at all, for the world does not even suspect their existence. Jesus said that the yeast must be hidden in the bottom of the trough of dough in order that it may work night and day in silence until fermentation of the entire mass has taken place.

An initiate can then with simplicity and sincerity practice the religion into which he was born, for all rites diversely represent one and the same dogma. But no initiate should open the depths of his conscience except to God, nor give account of his most intimate beliefs to anyone. The priest cannot judge that which the Pope himself cannot understand. The exterior signs of the initiate are modest knowledge, philanthropy without show, equality of character and the most inalterable goodness.

Yours in the holy science,

Eliphas Lévi

www.ingramcontent.com/pod-product-compliance
Lightning Source LLC
Chambersburg PA
CBHW071752090426
42738CB00011B/2659